Beautifully Broken
and
Righteously Restored

ANGELA KISELA

ISBN 979-8-89243-446-1 (paperback)
ISBN 979-8-89243-447-8 (digital)

Copyright © 2024 by Angela Kisela

All rights reserved. No part of this publication may be reproduced, distributed, or transmitted in any form or by any means, including photocopying, recording, or other electronic or mechanical methods without the prior written permission of the publisher. For permission requests, solicit the publisher via the address below.

Christian Faith Publishing
832 Park Avenue
Meadville, PA 16335
www.christianfaithpublishing.com

All Bible references were taken from the King James Version of the Holy Bible unless otherwise stated.

Printed in the United States of America

PRELUDE

One can take the broken pieces of their life and attempt to glue them back into place with the adhesive the world offers. However, this method always has the same result, which is the crumbling of the pieces once again, from the reverberating of the loudest roar or the blowing of the fiercest wind.

Occasionally, one will take the shattered pieces, beautifully broken, and lay them into the master's hand. He will then, ever so gently, adhere them back into place, and they will be forever righteously restored.

CHAPTER 1

Cassie's Cross

Silently, Cassie sat beside the cross, holding a Michelob in one hand and a Marlboro in the other. She kept contemplating whether or not she should get closer to the tall wooden monument that loomed before her. This wasn't the first time Cassie had come to the cross. Each time she would muster up the courage to approach, she would make it thus far and then stop. She just wasn't ready yet. She wasn't good enough yet. She clung tightly to the glass bottle. How could she quit drinking? It was her only escape from the harshness of hell that she called reality. Her cigarette dangled between her lips as she sucked in its poison. The warmth of it calmed her nerves. How could she ever kneel before such a sacred statue the way she was?

"This was stupid," she said aloud and rose to her feet. The weight of her chains was almost too heavy to bear. Someone ran past her, knocking her down. Cassie could smell his stench. It was the stench of death. He was so dirty, and his clothes were tattered and worn.

"Hey!" she shouted. The man did not seem to see or hear her. Cassie watched as he flung himself violently onto the cross. His chains wrapped around the cross from the impact of his thrust. His dirty fingers were gripping the beauty of the cross and staining it with his filth.

"I can't do it!" the man screamed in torment. "I can't handle it anymore! Please! Take it!" He reached into his pockets and pulled green pieces of paper from them. It was money! Cassie sat in amazement as the man threw money at the cross. What? Did he think he could buy his way to heaven?

The man fell to his knees. A picture of a naked woman fell from his fingers. "I can't stop looking at them. Please, take them too."

Cassie just shook her head as she pondered her thoughts. She realized that she was wrong. The man wasn't trying to buy his way anywhere. He was simply giving his money to the cross. *Interesting*, she thought. *Why would someone do that?*

The cross, which was wrapped with the chains of the man and the grime from his fingers, was now beginning to glow. Cassie stared intently. At first, she thought she was losing her mind. A white light illuminated the entire area where the man knelt. The items that he had placed before the cross disappeared into the ground. His chains fell off as if someone had come along and sliced them in two! When the man stood up, all the dirt that adorned his body simply fell off. He was clean. He was handsome. He hugged the cross and then turned and walked toward Cassie.

The man reached out his hand and helped her up. "I'm sorry that I knocked you down. I was desperate. I needed help."

Cassie didn't know what to say. Her anger with the man subsided. She felt happy for him. He appeared to be a changed man. She clutched her bottle behind her back. Her chains clanked against it.

"Don't wait. You should go now. Just like this." The man turned and ran.

What did he know? How dare he tell her what to do? She endured enough of that in her lifetime. She was sick and tired of people, especially men, telling her what to do.

Cassie heard the clanking of someone else's chains and turned around to see a beautiful young woman with long golden hair that cascaded all the way down her back. Her eyes were bright and blue and reminded Cassie of a picture she saw once of the ocean. The young woman's chains seemed to sparkle. Cassie wondered why on earth the young woman was even there. Surely, she was perfect. How could she possibly need anything the cross could give her?

The young woman held her hand toward the cross. Cassie could see a beautiful silver mirror between the young woman's fingers. Cassie watched as the young woman threw the mirror at the cross and fell to her knees, sobbing. Cassie felt compassion for her. As Cassie began to walk toward the young woman to offer some form of comfort, she noticed the young woman's reflection in the mirror.

"Ah!" Cassie gasped; her hands flew over her mouth. The image was repulsive. The reflection was grayish in color, with veins protruding all around the section where the young woman's nose should've been. Pieces of flesh were missing from the cheekbones. The lips were completely absent from her face. Only yellow pieces of jagged teeth remained. The image reminded Cassie of a zombie movie from her younger days.

Cassie kept glancing back and forth from the beautiful young woman that she saw before her to the grotesque figure reflected in the mirror. The young girl crawled to the foot of the cross and lay for what seemed like hours. Cassie wanted to leave. She wanted to give this young woman her own space and time at the cross, but she just couldn't walk away. Cassie had never seen someone so beautiful on the outside but so horrific looking on what appeared to be the inside. The glowing of the cross interrupted Cassie's thoughts.

Had Cassie not already witnessed a miraculous transformation from the man before, she wouldn't have believed her eyes. The glow of the cross engulfed the young woman. Cassie could see the reflection from the mirror that still lay on the ground. Tears filled her eyes as she watched the face of Christ replace the gruesome one before it. When the young woman climbed to her feet, Cassie noticed that her chains were gone. The young woman threw her hands in the air and started singing "Amazing Grace" as she walked away.

Cassie could feel the cross beckoning to her once again. She stepped back a little farther, hiding the bottle and cigarette from its view. Her own chains felt heavier than they did before. She sat down. The night began to fall. Cassie sipped from the bottle and inhaled more of the poisonous vapor that dangled between her fingers. A few more drags, and then she'd quit. Maybe. Then she'd approach the cross herself. Maybe.

Sleep found Cassie as the sky drew darker. She dreamed of a time when she was younger and happier. A time before she ran away from home. A time before she started selling her body to men. But oh, the money! The money was so good! Unfortunately, nothing lasts forever. Not even money. Cassie had left the streets and found a house for young, battered women. She couldn't believe the heartache that some of them had to bear.

Cassie had thought her home life was bad. She only ran away because she never got her way. Not because someone was hurting her. Not because she wasn't loved. Cassie tried to go home once. She even walked to the door and rang the bell. But someone else answered. An elderly man who told her the sad story of the family who had died in a car crash. He bought the house from a sheriff's auction. Now Cassie was completely alone. She couldn't go home. She couldn't go back to the streets. So she waitressed at a local bar and worked part-time at a tattoo parlor. Cassie was quite good with the ink pen. Her own arms were covered with roses and vines.

The commotion woke Cassie from her slumber. She sat up. Two men stood before the cross, fighting. One man was dressed in a business suit and the other in simple jeans and a red shirt. The man in jeans clung to the man in the suit as if trying to prevent him from stepping closer to the cross.

"You can't do this! We are meant to be!"

"No!" The man in the suit yelled back, struggling to break free.

"We are perfect for each other! How can you do this to us?"

"No! We're not! I was wrong. I was so very wrong! I'm sorry!" screamed the man, still trying to escape the other's grasp.

"No! Don't do it!" The man in the red shirt began to beg the other.

The man in the suit was more determined because Cassie watched as he screamed again and then threw himself at the foot of the cross. But then, the man in the red shirt took his chains, threw them around the man in the suit, and tried pulling him away. But the other man prayed, "Lord! I'm so sorry! Please—help me!"

Cassie's eyes widened in awe as she witnessed two huge men dressed in silver armor emerge from the cross and grab the man in the red shirt. Cassie knew they were angels. There was no doubt in her mind as she watched them carry the man in the red shirt away from the man at the cross. The angels then went back to the man in the suit and helped him up. This time, the cross glowed so brightly that Cassie had to look away. When she did, she noticed a woman and two children off in the distance. Their heads were bowed, and they were holding hands. Cassie wondered what they were doing there. Cassie also noticed that none of them had chains.

The man in the suit stepped away from the cross. His chains were gone, and his suit glistened. Cassie could hear the angels rejoicing, singing, "Glory to God! The One who IS and WAS and IS to come! For only HE can rescue man from the lusts of their flesh." Cassie began to cry as the man ran to the woman and children. They all fell to their knees in the most beautiful embrace Cassie had ever seen. She could almost feel their relief and love. Their love was so strong!

Cassie desperately longed for someone to love her that way. But there was no one left to love her. She watched the family walk away, and the cross once again stopped glowing. Cassie sat back down. She was too tired to leave and too awake to sleep. What an amazing day she had witnessed. If only everyone knew how incredible this cross was, then everyone would want to come to it.

"Are you ready, Cassie?" she heard a soft voice speak.

Cassie looked around. There was darkness everywhere. "Who's there?"

"You are looking for peace, are you not? For freedom from the chains that bind you?"

"What? How do you know that?" Cassie rose to her feet. Who was speaking to her? She still couldn't see anyone.

"I know all about you, Cassie. I created you."

"Ha!" Cassie blurted. "Now that's funny." She continued laughing. "If you made me, then I bet you are pretty disappointed in this masterpiece of yours." She kept laughing.

"I'm not disappointed in you, Cassie. I love you."

Cassie's laughter trailed off. Tears began to roll down her cheeks. "So what are you, like God or something?"

"I am"

"Well, what do you want from me? I'm upset with you, you know! How could you let me run away from home? How could you let my family die?" Cassie's tears turned to anger. If this was God, she had a few things to get off her chest.

"I never told you to run away, Cassie."

"But you didn't try to stop me! And look what happened! Do you know what I had to do to survive? Of course, you know. You're *God*," Cassie said sarcastically.

"I'm sorry that you didn't choose the road I had planned for you, Cassie. You chose your own way. But I was still there beside you. I was crying with you when you were hurting. I was holding your hand when you felt alone. I have never left you. I was waiting for the time when you would visit me. This isn't your first time here. Every time you would come to see me, I would get so excited. But then you would walk away."

Cassie wasn't about to fall for this crap. "What about my family! How can a loving God let my family die! Now I have no one!" Cassie began to cry. Gut-wrenching, heartbreaking sobs escaped her lips.

"You have me, Cassie."

This time, Cassie put down her drink and took the last puff of her cigarette. She wiped her eyes and looked up. There before her was a man, simply dressed in a white robe. He held out his hand to her.

"Follow me, Cassie. I promise to take care of you. I know you are weary. I will give you rest."

Cassie just stared at his hands. She wanted desperately to reach out and take them. But how could she? Could it be true? Could he really love her and want to take care of her? Her chains were heavy and laden with guilt and despair and so much heartache. She almost couldn't meet his grasp. Then he bent down and put his arms under Cassie's legs and around her shoulders. In one quick movement, she was in his arms. God was carrying her. Oh no! She was going to ruin him! She wasn't good enough to come to the cross yet. What was she doing?

She hid her face in his shoulder, and he read her thoughts.

"You cannot ruin me, Cassie. Don't be afraid. I love you. If you let me, I can heal you."

Cassie tried gazing at his face, but it was so bright. His whole being poured out love, grace, and comfort. The closer he carried Cassie to the cross, the more overwhelmed she became. Then he put her down.

"What are you doing?" she asked. Her disappointment was evident.

"It must be your choice, Cassie. I can only carry you so far. You must choose to follow me. Will you follow me, Cassie?"

Cassie could feel the weight of her chains again. All the torment was back.

"But—" she began.

"No. There are no excuses, Cassie. You must decide. Will you choose me and the life I have planned for you?"

"Well, if I do, will you promise that I'll never be sad again?"

Jesus looked into her very soul. His next words stirred something deep within her she didn't even know she had. "No. I cannot promise you that it will be easy. But I promise to be there to take the worst before it comes to you. I promise to fill your heart with peace that will go beyond your understanding. And I promise, Cassie, to carry you throughout the times you think you cannot walk. I will strengthen you. I will uphold you. I will never leave you or forsake you. This peace and joy that I will give you, the world cannot take away. So long as you walk with me."

Cassie knew he meant every word he spoke. She could feel it radiating through her heart. She had never stood this close to the cross before. All it would take was one small step for her to reach out and place her hand upon it. What did she have to lose except the terrible burden that became her rusted chains? She knew there was no going back. And for once, she was okay with that.

With every ounce of strength that ran through her veins, Cassie stepped forward and fell into the arms of her Savior. The glow of the cross wrapped itself around them, and Cassie cried out as her chains were ripped away.

Forever gone.

God was right.

She could not begin to understand this peace that now replaced her heartache. This joy ran through her veins where torment once lived. Why had she waited so long to come to the cross! Cassie opened her eyes and saw she stood alone. But she knew she wasn't alone. She could feel the love of her Savior. She wore a long white dress. She was free.

"Thank you," Cassie said and began her journey home.

Someone stood in the distance. Cassie could see an elderly man dressed in suspenders and an old white T-shirt. His chains were old and grimy. As she drew closer, she recognized him. He was the man who lived in her old house.

"Hello," she said. She wondered what he was doing there.

"I'm sorry. I am so very sorry. I lied to you. I was drunk when you came to the door. I just wanted you to go away. I didn't want to be bothered. But as soon as you left, I felt so terrible that I had to follow you…to give you this."

Cassie reached out her hand and took an envelope from him. It smelled of liquor.

Cassie looked at him and then tore the envelope open. Tears fell upon the words:

> Dear Cassie,
>
> If you are reading this, then you are alive, and we are so grateful! We have prayed every minute since you left us for your return. Your dad lost his job, and we had to move to another town to find work. We are not far away! Here is our new address.
>
> Please, please, please, come home.
>
> Love,
> Mom

"I'm sorry. I'm so sorry." The man's apology was interrupted by Cassie's arms wrapped around his neck. She was hugging him.

The elderly man was not expecting this type of response. He didn't know what to say. He smiled at her and watched her walk away. She was almost glowing.

He looked at the cross that stood in the distance.

He picked up his chains and walked toward it.

CHAPTER 2

Sara's Scars

Sara drew her knees into her chest and sobbed. The steel blade so often used to pierce her flesh lay patiently beside her. It's silver smile begged her to wrap her fingers around it.

Sara's arms and legs were covered with remembrances of past circumstances she simply could not handle. She longed to possess the courage to make it all go away. Just one quick slit is all it would take. One vertical slice at the wrist, and she could close her eyes forever.

The truth was that Sara should have never been born. Literally. Her mother was told she could never have children. Free birth control. But her mother *did* conceive, and into the world came Sara. A miracle to some but a nuisance to most. At least Sara perceived herself as such. Nuisance. Mistake.

Sara's childhood was filled with inappropriate touching and situations best covered on the ten o'clock news. Until her Nana and Papa stepped in. One steadfast swoop snatched Sara from her bed of devastation into the arms of unconditional love. It was there Sara was taught the truth of her miraculous existence. She truly was a miracle. Yet no matter how many Sundays Nana and Papa dragged her to church, the pain remained.

If there was a God, and that was a big *if*, how dare he allow all the monstrosities to wreak havoc on her early years? If he truly loved her, he would have prevented the horrific encounters from ever taking place. But he did not. He stood on the sidelines and apparently watched since he was *omniscient*, as they said. So sure, she believed in him, and she disliked him tremendously.

Nana would kneel at the end of Sara's bed. Hands clasped tightly, she would pray for Sara's heart to open and allow the light of the Lord to engulf her. Sara often questioned Nana.

"Why do you always kneel beside my bed and talk to yourself?"

"I'm not talking to myself, Sara. I'm talking to God."

"God? Why him?"

It broke Nana's heart that Sara doubted the Savior.

"I don't like him. Please do not talk to him anymore. Not in here. Not in my room."

Nana never prayed in Sara's room after that. But she did pray everywhere else whenever she could.

Sara's high school years began with the news of her mother's death. An overdose. Sara barely knew her, yet she felt sadness for Nana and Papa. Sara knew they loved her mother. During Sara's senior year, her Papa was diagnosed with cancer. Soon, after Papa went home—they called it—Nana got sick and died too.

Sara had endured so much in her young life that one would think she would have lost her mind. Maybe she did. She was enrolled in her second semester of college. But Sara fought the urge to abuse the cocaine and heroin that presented themselves to her at every college party. In fact, even the alcohol desperately tried latching onto her soul. *Nice try, Whiskey. You are not my poison*, she would joke when her friends taunted her with it.

No, Sara's poison stood tall with broad shoulders and blue-green eyes. Blake had a football scholarship. One day, he would become an all-star quarterback. Nothing and no one would stand in his way. Not even an unexpected pregnancy.

"Just get rid of it! My god! How could you do this to me! I thought you were on the pill?"

"I was. I am! But it's not full proof!"

"Well, you have to get rid of it. I cannot be a dad. I cannot take care of a baby, Sara."

Those five words: *Just. Get. Rid. Of. It.* Five simple words that echoed in Sara's heart.

Blake drove her to the clinic. He gave her the money for the procedure and left. That was the last time Sara saw him. Sara sat in the waiting room and held the signed papers so tightly in her hands, her knuckles aching. Nana and Papa would be so disappointed if they knew she was there. They thought children were gifts from God. They thought she was a gift from God.

Sara was twelve when she accidentally cut her finger on a knife. For a moment, the pain was intense. Then quietly, it began to seep out of her heart through her blood into the realm of relief. Ache and sadness hitched a ride. For a little while, she was whole again. Sara learned this technique required practice. Her arms and legs were the ideal place to make the tiny incisions. Sara could easily hide the evidence beneath her clothes.

"The truth always makes itself known," Nana proclaimed with tears in her eyes and a swift grip on Sara's wrist. Up went Sara's sleeve to reveal what Nana had prayed was not the case. "Sara! Sweetheart. What have you been doing to yourself! Don't you know what a gift you are? What a blessing you have been for me and Papa? God loves you so much. He does not want you to hurt yourself. He wants you to love yourself because he loves you."

"Leave me alone!" Sara wiggled free. "You don't understand anything!"

"Oh, honey, but I do."

"No, you don't!" Sara had run outside into the yard and cried. She felt so worthless. So pathetic. Even the quail seemed to tease her. Sara could hear their call: *You're. So. Stupid. You're. So. Stupid. You're. So. Stupid.*

Sara caused Nana and Papa such pain. She wished she could go back and never leave her parents. Maybe then she would have ended up dead, which is where she belonged. There was no way she was having this baby. No way. Yet as she said those words to her heart, her feet made their way out of the clinic toward home.

Sara stretched out her hand and placed her shaky fingers on the silver blade. She carefully began to push against her skin. "Come on. You can do this."

But she could not. Not there. Not in her room. Sara stood up and made her way down the hall. She would end her life in the bathroom. It would be easier that way for whoever found her.

Sara had to pass Nana and Papa's room. She paused. She touched the door, not intending for it to open. But it did. The smell of love and warm embraces engulfed her senses. What was she doing in there? She had not ventured into their room since they had died. Nana and Papa left the house to Sara in their will. Sara was grateful the mortgage had long been paid and a trust fund had enough to cover her college tuition, along with any living expenses that arose. How could they love her so much? How could they give her so much when she deserved nothing? *Nothing.*

The waterfall of tears flowed fiercely from her eyes. She sat on the edge of the bed and slowly slid down to the floor. "God! What is wrong with YOU? Look at what you've done to me!" Sara flung her arms back. The knife escaped her grasp and disappeared under the bed. Sara tried to retrieve it, but instead, a small wooden box found its way into her hands. She blew the dust off and opened the hinged lid. Inside was a small book with a silver clasp. Sara wiped her eyes and began reading the words.

Dearest Diary,

> Today, he looked at me. He smiled. My heart melted. He was beautiful. His name is Phil. Tomorrow, he will ask me out. I just know it. I will say yes. We will live happily ever after.

Phil? Who was Phil? Her Papa was Charles. Sara never knew Nana loved someone before Papa. The two of them had been married for over fifty years. Who had time for someone else? Sara felt as if she was invading Nana's privacy. Yet she had to learn more about Nana's life before Papa. The entries painted a wonderful picture of two people in love, getting ready to start a life together—until they did not.

> Dearest Diary,
>
> Tonight is the night. I am going to give myself to Phil. I know that he loves me. I know this will make him see that I love him too. He does not mean to be cruel when he drinks. I know I can change him.

Nana! What was she thinking! Sara kept reading. Nana had given herself to Phil, and Phil had gone from a charming prince to a terrible troll!

> Dearest Diary,
>
> Phil did not mean to hit me. But it did hurt terribly so. What will I tell Mamma? How can I hide these bruises? And there is something else. Something that I cannot speak of. It is terrible.

Sara searched the following entries to try and decipher what was so terrible. What happened to her nana?

> Dearest Diary,
>
> I have nothing left to live for. Phil has left me. He has ruined me. No other man will want me. I do not know what I will do. So I will pray. I will talk to God. Mamma always said God loved me. Maybe I will ask him to save me. I will ask him to forgive me for having this abortion. But if he does not, then there is nothing left to do… but close my eyes forever.

Sara gasped. How could this be? How could Nana feel so helpless? Nana had an abortion. Sara's heart broke. There were so many pages that were ripped from the binding. Chapters of Nana's life that were unaccounted for. What did that mean? The entries that remained were different now.

Dearest Diary,

>Today, I became Mrs. Charles Pierce. I have never been so happy. He has a wonderful son named William. I will love them both with all my heart. I am so thankful to the Lord for saving me and giving me a second chance at love. Even though I cannot bear children of my own, I will love William as if he were mine.

Sara was putting the pieces together. She never knew William did not belong to Nana. Nana loved him so much. She always talked about him as if he were her son. Nana wanted Sara to know William and how wonderful he was. How much he loved her mother.

Dearest Diary,

>Once again, I am in mourning. My heart shattered today. William has gone home to be with the Lord. There was an accident. His girlfriend survived. Thankfully, so did their unborn child. The doctors said Patricia is having a baby girl. Patricia is devastated. She confided in me that she was not supposed to be able to conceive. We promised her we would help take care of them both. We were overjoyed at the miracle before us.

And then,

> Dearest Diary,
>
> Today, Patricia gave birth to the most beautiful baby girl that I have ever seen. Charles and I adore her. Patricia has found a nice young man who wants to marry her. We are very happy.
>
> Dearest Dairy,
>
> It has been so long since I have used your pages to express the cries of my heart. So much is different. Patricia has allowed drugs to change her into someone we no longer recognize. The young man has turned into three. She is so lost. We are praying for her. We are praying for Sara. We know something is not right. We are doing all that we can to get custody of her. We have faith we will succeed.

Sara flipped through the entries. She was saddened by her mother's choices. The boyfriends. The root causes of Sara's pain. Sara felt pity for her mother. Sara wished she had known Patricia before she was lost.

The rest of the entries were not titled Dearest Diary. They were prayers.

> Lord,
>
> Today, Sara asked me to stop talking to you in her room. I am so sorry. Of course, I will still pray every chance I get. I will not stop. One day, she will be praying too. I just know it.

Lord,

>Today, I discovered Sara's scars. She has them all over her arms and even her legs. However, she does not know that I know about her legs. Please help her. She does not want anything to do with you. She says she does not like you. But she does not know the real you. Only the idea of who she thinks you are.

Sara flipped through the prayers. Nana loved God so much. So many prayers for people that Nana knew. Her friends. People at the grocery store. Prayers for Sara. The thought of someone, God, loving Sara was almost unbelievable.

Lord,

>Today, Charles found out what has been making him so ill. It is cancer. We have not tested me, but I know my diagnosis will be similar. We do not think Sara can handle both of us being sick, so we decided to keep mine quiet. We know that you have a plan. We trust it. When it is time for us to go home, we will leave the house and all our assets to Sara. The trust fund that we created for her will be available when she becomes an adult. We pray that it will be enough for her.

Sara sobbed. How could Nana and Papa keep that from her? Sara just thought that Nana got sick and gave up. She had no idea Nana had cancer too. Oh! If only Sara had shown how much she appreciated them! But she had not. Sara was so self-absorbed in her own victim mentality that she did not see the pain others were experiencing.

> Lord,
>
> Charles has gone home to be with you, and I know, soon, you will call me too. I have all the legalities straightened out. Sara will be fine. But she needs you. Please guide her. I know she will be hesitant to talk to you. But when she does, please, please, please listen with your whole heart. I pray that every day, something happens in her life that makes her question her unbelief. I have faith that one day, I will see her again.

That was Nana's last entry. Sara stood up. Nana's dresser was untouched. The oval mirror above it reflected someone Sara no longer wanted to be. "God, are you there? If so, I need to talk to you."

Sara waited for a moment, unsure what she was expecting. Him to respond to her? She shook her head. She stared at her image. She was twenty-two years old and lived a life filled with pain and stupidity. She unbuttoned her blouse to reveal the trail of scars that were now mapped across her abdomen. What had she done to herself? Subconsciously, she began to rub the area where her unborn child grew. Was it possible that she could raise a child? How could she love a child if she could not love herself?

"God? I am sorry that I yelled at you before." Sara sighed heavily. "It's just that. Well, if you are so good and so loving, how could you let all the bad things happen? How could you take Nana and Papa away from me? Especially if you knew that I'd become pregnant?"

Sara's anger returned. Seriously? How could he? What was she to do? She tapped the dresser and intended to walk away when her shirt got caught in the drawer. It opened just enough for her to see Nana's Bible inside. She picked it up with shaky hands. Its brown leather cover was soft to the touch, worn from use. It was barely held together. Sara carefully turned the pages. So many parts were highlighted.

> For God so loved the world, that he gave his only begotten Son, that whosoever believeth in him should not perish, but have everlasting life. (John 3:16)
>
> For all have sinned, and come short of the glory of God. (Romans 3:23)
>
> For the wages of sin is death; but the gift of God is eternal life through Jesus Christ our Lord. (Romans 6:23)
>
> For I am persuaded, that neither death, nor life, nor angels, nor principalities, nor powers, nor things present, nor things to come, Nor height, nor depth, nor any other creature, shall be able to separate us from the love of God, which is in Christ Jesus our Lord. (Romans 8:38–39)
>
> That if thou shalt confess with thy mouth the Lord Jesus, and shalt believe in thine heart that God hath raised him from the dead, thou shalt be saved. (Romans 10:9)
>
> Verily, verily, I say unto you, He that heareth my word, and believeth on him that sent me, hath everlasting life, and shall not come into condemnation; but is passed from death unto life. (John 5:24)

Sara's heart began to soften. Perhaps there was hope for her after all. Nana believed this book to be truth. The more Sara read, the more things began to fit together. It didn't all make sense to her, but there was this feeling, this strange emotion that began to fill her heart. It was belief. Sara closed the book and held it to her chest. If God did love her that much, like Nana said, then Sara would give him a chance.

Just then, Sara heard the quail chirping. *"I love you. I love you. I love you."* Sara finally believed that he did.

CHAPTER 3

Heidi's Heartache

"Heidi Peterson, to the principal's office."

It was a simple command. Yet Heidi's insides felt as though they would leak into her shoes if she stood up. If she stood up, she would need to walk to the front of the room and then escape out the door. She could try and avoid rows two and three, where Alex sat in the third seat from the front, but that would result in her almost sideswiping Melanie's desk as she bolted to the door.

"Take a deep breath, honey. Focus on one thing. One task. Slowly breathe out. You can do this." Her mother's words echoed in her ear.

"Heidi?" Her teacher broke her concentration. "You'll need to go to the office."

Heidi nodded. She collected her things and made her way to the door. *One step. Two steps. One breath. Two breaths.* She made it safely to the hallway.

Mr. Branson was waiting at the door for Heidi. "Come on in."

Heidi sat down. The butterflies in her stomach were relentless. She was going to vomit.

Mr. Branson interrupted her thoughts. "Heidi. How are you doing today? Are you feeling okay?"

Heidi had been dealt her share of tragedies. Her mother passed away last spring, and her grandmother the winter before. All Heidi had left was her father.

"I'm doing alright, Mr. Branson. Thanks for asking. How are you?"

Mr. Branson folded his hands on the desk. A heavy sigh reverberated through his shoulders. "Heidi. I wish I wasn't the one to tell you this. But I'm afraid we haven't been able to track another family member down yet."

The butterflies flew into Heidi's intestines, ramming her from the inside out. They made their way to her throat. She couldn't breathe. She couldn't speak. She could only hear what he said next.

"I'm so sorry, Heidi, but there's been a terrible accident. I'm afraid your father was killed at work. There was an explosion…"

She could not bear it anymore. Her earthshattering scream caused Heidi to cover her ears as shards of glass from the windows cut at her arms.

"Heidi?" Mr. Branson brought her back to reality. There was no broken glass. Only pieces of her broken heart were on the floor.

Heidi could not recall much after that day. There was a funeral. The casket was closed. No way for her to say goodbye. Most of the world was fuzzy now. Heidi stayed with the neighbor until Heidi's aunt, a woman Heidi had never met, flew in from somewhere to take her home. Heidi's beautiful round face was stained with tears. Her strawberry blond strands were matted to the sides of her cheeks. She did not care. Her devotional sat next to her bed. She picked it up and threw it at the wall. Heidi got up to finish it off. She would shred that book if she did nothing else today. Bending, she noticed the scripture. Her mother often quoted it when her grandmother passed away.

> The righteous cry, and the LORD heareth, and delivereth them out of all their troubles. The LORD is nigh unto them that are of a broken heart; and saveth such as be of a contrite spirit. (Psalm 34:17–18)

Heidi lost track of time. She kept repeating the verses. Over and over. Aloud and in her head. Just like her mother instructed her to do. *"Heidi. It's alright to be overwhelmed. Emotions are good for us. But we must not let them get the upper hand. We are in control of them, not the other way around. Let's read some more."*

Heidi's mother was a firm believer in the power of prayer and scripture. *"The more you fill yourself with Scripture, the less room there is for doubt, fear, or anxiety."*

Heidi recited the words now, but the power that once filled her soul when she spoke them now exhausted her vocal cords. Heidi couldn't understand how such a loving God could allow such terrible things. If someone had to die, why not her? She was the one struggling so much from the passing of her grandmother and then her mother. Two women she never thought she could live without. The death of her mother caused a chemical imbalance, the doctors said. Heidi could barely pronounce the names of the drugs she was taking. All she knew was they made her feel like a zombie. So she stopped taking them.

"Heidi, what were you thinking? You can't just stop taking these. There is a reason you need them. They will help you." Her father scolded her when he realized she'd stopped.

"I would rather feel pain and sadness than nothing at all." Oh, how times change. Now Heidi didn't care if she ever felt anything again.

The storm came through in the middle of the night and knocked out the power. Heidi opened her eyes. Darkness. She rolled over to her side to see a glimpse of light beneath the door. Curious, she felt her way to the door and opened it. She could hear faint voices down the hall.

"That's fine. I can sleep on the couch and in the morning. I'll take her home." A soft voice spoke.

"I'll get you a blanket. I think it's wonderful that you're doing this."

Heidi wished she could see who it was. Yawning, she felt her way back to her room.

The sun broke through the crack in the curtains, and Heidi wiped the sleep from her eyes. Reality was a bully that Heidi hated. She wanted to fight back and call it names. To punch it straight in the throat. But she knew it was pointless.

Downstairs, Heidi came upon a head of fiery red curls. The creature must have sensed Heidi's presence because, just as Heidi approached, she turned over. The most beautiful brown eyes stared at Heidi. "Good morning, sweetie."

Heidi replied, "Good morning."

"You must be Heidi." She extended her hand.

"Yes. Who are you?"

"My name is Lynn. I'm your aunt."

Heidi heard a story once of her dad's sister who moved to England. There was some family drama of which she knew not the details.

"I am here to take you home."

Heidi stared into the pools of chocolate that smiled back at her. Lynn stood up. She was tall and strong. Lynn reached out and hugged Heidi. Heidi instantly felt safe.

"I know that we haven't met before this, and I'm so sorry that we have to meet for the first time…under these very…sad…circumstances."

"Thank you. Where will we go?" Heidi hoped it was somewhere far, far away.

"Well, I did live in England. But I moved to Colorado. I live in a beautiful town named Evergreen. I live there with Toby."

"Toby? Is he your husband?'

Lynn laughed. "No. Toby is my Pitbull. He's a brilliant little dog."

Heidi smiled. She had always wanted to own a dog.

"See." Lynn pulled out her phone and showed Heidi a picture. The cutest little black dog with sad eyes stared back. "Toby is going to love you."

The days that followed were a whirlwind of emotions. The flight was long and gave Heidi time to think. The more she thought, the more her insides twisted. How would she go on? How could she live with a stranger? An aunt that she had never known before. How could her parents specify that in their will? Why was Lynn not as heartbroken as Heidi? Lynn did lose her brother, after all. Nothing made sense.

"Heidi? Are you alright?" Heidi felt safe with this woman, but Lynn didn't know Heidi's heartache. She didn't understand what she had to deal with every day. Lynn reached out her hand and placed it on Heidi's. A sense of calm came over Heidi. "I know this must be scary for you. But I promise. It will all be okay."

Heidi closed her eyes and counted until she drifted off to sleep.

A white two-story house sitting on six beautiful acres of land welcomed Heidi. An open stairway led to the second floor, where Lynn showed Heidi her room. Two French doors opened onto a balcony overlooking the garden. Heidi's eyes danced. A plush chair sat next to a bookshelf filled with books.

"Do you like to read, Heidi?" Lynn walked up beside her.

Heidi looked up at her aunt. "I love to read."

"Well, you are welcome to read whatever you like. My home is now your home."

"Thank you." Heidi wrapped her arms around her aunt.

Could this be true? Could this wonderful woman really mean to take care of her?

Lynn hugged Heidi with strength and love. "Heidi, you needn't be worried. I'll take care of you."

Heidi's life was turned upside down so many times in the last few years. She was almost afraid to breathe a sigh of relief. But she did. She took a deep breath and let it out slowly. Maybe things would be better now. Or not.

Heidi walked up the stairs of the brick building. No matter how far away you run from your problems, you never really escape. The problems are always lurking behind the next hallway, ready to stick their feet out just as you walk past so that you fall, face-first, into the pool of embarrassment. Heidi's old school showcased two major bullies: Alex and Melanie. Now it seemed this school was no different. Janice and Terrie led a group of girls into chaos and disruptions. Heidi's locker was just in between them both.

"Hey there, new girl." Janice spoke. "Welcome to our school. Now if you don't want trouble, hand over your phone."

The room started to spin. Heidi's lungs began to shrivel. She clutched her books to her chest. This was what a heart attack felt like. It had to be. The pain was brief, sharp, and right between her shoulder blades. Beads of sweat formed on her brow.

"Remember. One breath. Two breaths. Your problems are big, but God is bigger. Focus on what you know. And what do you know, Heidi?" her mother's voice echoed.

I know that I'm going to die right here, right now, Heidi thought.

She remembered her mother's voice, *"Heidi. What do you know?"*

Heidi took a deep breath and let it out slowly. "*I know that I can do all things through Christ which strentheneth me."*

"Hey, weirdo. Yoo-hoo! Earth to new kid." Janice interrupted her memory.

"Janice, don't be so mean so soon. She doesn't know our policies yet," Terrie added.

Heidi took a step back. "My name is Heidi. I don't have a phone." She tried to sound stern.

Janice stuck out her foot. Heidi dropped her books to catch her fall, revealing sweat stains beneath her arms.

"Ew! Gross." Both girls poked fun at Heidi.

Heidi gathered her things and ran to the restroom. She threw herself into a stall and slid to the floor. Heidi sat there, waiting to die.

Heidi couldn't recall how long she was on the floor. Her face was soaked with tears. Her head was pounding. Wads of toilet paper were scattered on the floor. Why did she ever think that her life would be better? Both parents and her grandma were now gone. Yes, she knew she would see them again one day, but she wanted desperately for that day to be now. She couldn't do it. She could not face the bullies who tormented her everywhere she went. If it wasn't an Alex or a Janice, it would be the crowd at the mall or the teacher making her recite a poem in front of the class. Life was just too hard.

The sound of the door opening interrupted Heidi's pity party. "Heidi? Are you in here?"

It was Lynn.

Heidi wiped her tears as her aunt waited for her to unlatch the door. Heidi flung herself into Lynn's open arms.

"Can we go home?" Heidi cried.

Lynn knelt and peered into Heidi's innocent eyes. "Well, that's up to you. We can go home, and you can crawl into bed and worry and fret all the while life is slipping through your fingers, minutes and new memories at a time. Or you can wipe your tears and walk right into your next class, head held high with a smile on your face—because you are Heidi. You can face anything."

Heidi bowed her head. "What if I can't face anything?"

"Then I guess we will head home until you can."

Heidi stayed home that last semester of seventh grade and all of eighth. She finished her classes online. Her summers were spent helping Lynn tend to the garden and playing with Toby. Her first winter in Colorado was filled with snowball fights, skiing, and, of course, reading. Heidi filled herself up with as much Christian literature as possible. She followed the everyday heroes through their tortuous lives. The struggles they faced were so harsh, so real, so close to how Heidi felt most of the time. Overwhelmed with fear and anxiety. Just when they thought the end was near, a ray of hope would shine through the darkness. Oh, how Heidi longed for her own happy ending.

Days turned into months and months to years, and before Heidi could make any more excuses, junior year was about to start. She was enrolled. She was packed. She was physically ready to attend classes. Emotionally, she was screaming inside a padded room, begging for anyone to open the door.

The yellow bus honked its horn, and Heidi reluctantly climbed aboard.

Focus. Focus. Look around. Breathe. Find a seat. She coaxed her feet to move.

There he sat. Seat twelve. Blond hair, half covering his eyes. Green eyes that looked up and met Heidi's. The corners of his lips pulled upward toward his cheeks. He was smiling at her!

Heidi hurriedly sat down in the front. She must have imagined him. She turned her head to the right over her shoulder. He was gone. He wasn't real.

"Hi."

Startled, Heidi whipped back around. He was there. He moved to sit in front of her.

"I'm Nick. Who are you?"

She couldn't speak. She pinched herself. Ouch! She was awake. He was really talking to her. "Hi. I'm Heidi."

"What year are you?"

Heidi couldn't help but smile back at him. "I'm a junior."

"I'm a junior too. I normally don't ride the bus, but my truck is in the shop. I'm picking it up after school today."

"You have a truck?"

"Sure do. Maybe I'll give you a ride sometime." And with that, he put his ear buds in and turned around, singing what Heidi thought was Christmas music.

This brick building was bigger than the last. It screamed at her as she approached the giant stairs. What was she thinking? She could not do this. No. She wasn't ready. Clutching her bag, she turned around to leave.

"Hey. Watch where you're going!" she smacked into someone. It couldn't be. It was *Janice*. "Well, if it isn't the cry baby."

Heidi was about to push past her when Nick reached out and grabbed her arm.

"Janice. Great to see you. Have you met my new best friend, Heidi?" He put his arm around her. Heidi couldn't breathe, but not from fear. Her heart was racing.

Janice stared at Heidi. "We've met before."

"Wonderful! Then I know if I'm not available and Heidi needs anything, you'll help her. Thanks so much." With that, he walked Heidi up the stairs and to her first class.

Heidi didn't dare look back at Janice, but she could feel daggers coming at her.

"Hey, listen. Janice acts like a bully, but she's not. She's just been through a lot. Try not to let her bother you, okay? Which lunch do you have?" he asked as he took her schedule. "Good. We have the same lunch. I'll see you then."

Heidi couldn't speak. What just happened? Was she dreaming? Was there really a knight who came and saved her from the fiery dragon?

The hours passed. Heidi needed to stop at her locker before heading to lunch. She shook her head. *Please don't be real*, she thought. There stood Janice. Her arms were full of books. She dreaded the thought of carrying them to lunch. *One step. Two steps. One breath. Two breaths.*

Heidi noticed Janice was staring at the locker next to hers. There were flower stickers placed all over the top half. Heidi opened her locker and put her books away. Janice looked as if she would cry. Heidi caught her gaze, and then Janice sneered and walked away.

Nick was waiting for her at lunch. He walked her to a table, and they sat down.

"Thank you for earlier today. For helping me."

"No need to thank me. I've been the new kid before. People are jerks sometimes, but you need to remember that everyone is battling something. Sometimes, the reason they are jerks is that they don't know how else to win their battle. It's not an excuse for them, but it's sometimes a reason. Regardless, you can't let them have power over you. You know, don't let them ruin your day." His smile was so bright.

Heidi felt herself smiling too.

"So what's your story?" Nick asked as he ate his sandwich.

"My story?"

"Yeah, you know. Where are you from, what do your parents do, et cetera?"

Heidi hung her head. "Ohio. I'm from Ohio. I moved here to live with my aunt."

"Oh. Were you a troublemaker? Did your parents send you away?" Nick joked.

"No. They, my parents, they both passed away."

"Oh, man. I'm sorry." Nick reached out and touched her hand. Heidi could feel the walls creep closer and closer to their table.

"Nick."

Heidi glanced up to see Janice.

"She's in my spot." Janice sat down next to Heidi.

Heidi scooted as far over as she could without falling off the seat. This day just needed to be over.

"Janice, there is plenty of room. I just learned that you and Heidi have something in common."

Heidi and Janice both looked at him. "I'll let you two figure it out." With those words, he grabbed his tray and walked away.

"What is he talking about?" Heidi asked Janice.

"I have no idea. He's random sometimes. You should know that since you're his new best friend."

"We just met today actually," Heidi admitted. She waited for Janice to turn on her.

"But of course, you did." Janice rolled her eyes and picked at her salad. Janice's phone sat face up on the table. A reminder popped up, and a picture of Janice and Terrie was shown as her background. Heidi noticed the sadness on Janice's face as she turned her phone over.

"That's a picture of your friend Terrie, right? I remember her from before—" Heidi stopped.

Janice stabbed at her tomatoes. "She's dead."

Heidi was not expecting Janice to respond with those words. A wave of empathy flooded over her. Heidi had never had a friend. Her mother and grandmother were the closest people to her. No one else understood her difficulties with certain situations in life.

"I'm so sorry."

Janice began to sob. Heidi placed her hand on Janice's shoulder. Janice wiped her eyes and shrugged. "Oh, stop it. Don't pretend to care."

Heidi wanted to yell at Janice and tell her that she wasn't the only person in pain.

"A quiet answer turneth away wrath," Her mother would say.

"I know you may not believe me, but I do understand the pain you are feeling. If you ever want to talk, I'm here to listen." Heidi stood up with her tray and walked away, tears streaming down her own face. This day needed to be over.

Nick sat next to Heidi on the bus ride home. "Why did you leave us at lunch?"

"Because I knew you could help her."

"What? Help Janice? With what?" Did Nick really believe she could help Janice? Heidi could barely wade through her own heartache, much less help someone else swim through theirs.

"Yes. I knew it this morning when we met. Right here on this bus. You have something within you. A light. A peace. Your eyes scream that you're in agony, but there's this strength about you."

Heidi glanced around. "Are you alright? I mean, surely you are not talking about me. You don't even know me."

"No. I don't. But I've seen that same look in your eyes in Janice's. Frankly, I don't know how to help her. None of us do. But then there was you. I just thought—"

"Well, don't think! You don't even know me, and I don't care how cute you are. You should not have done that!" Heidi's hands flew over her mouth.

"You think I'm cute?" Nick smiled.

Oh, Lord, kill me now. Why did I say that?

The bus came to her stop. She pushed past Nick, grateful to be away from him.

Ugh! The nerve! What was wrong with him? Who did he think he was?

*****

"Hey, sweetie! How was your first day?" Lynn greeted Heidi at the door. "Come on. Let's drink some tea on the patio, and you tell me all about it."

Heidi loved her aunt so much. She didn't understand why her parents never talked to Lynn. She loved the way her aunt listened as she complained about everything. Toby sat on Lynn's lap, listening too.

"Well, I'm sorry that you ran into the same girl who caused trouble for you from before. And I'm very sorry to hear that the other girl passed away. Do you know what happened?"

Heidi shook her head. "I didn't get the chance to ask. Nick thought it would be a good idea for me to help Janice through the pain of losing her best friend. He's obviously crazy."

Lynn smiled at Heidi. "Sweetie, I agree with Nick. You do have a sense of strength within you."

"I can barely help myself, Aunt Lynn. How could I possibly help someone else?"

"Just by being you."

"Well, I don't want to be like me. I wish I were like you."

"You are better than I ever could be, sweetie. You are just like your mother."

Lynn put Toby down and sat her tea aside. She leaned back and crossed her legs.

"I was going to wait to share this with you, but I think now is the time."

Heidi sat up straight. She had a feeling something big was about to be revealed.

"When I was in college, I met a man. Marcus. He was the light of my world. We were so happy. We were planning our wedding. Your father and he became fast friends. He asked your father to be his best man, and I asked your mother to be my maid of honor. We were all so excited.

"I found out I was pregnant a few months before the wedding." Lynn beamed. "On the day before the wedding, at the rehearsal dinner, your mother announced that she, too, was pregnant with you." Lynn smiled. "We talked all night about what we would name our children and how close you two would be." Lynn paused. "On the way home, there was an accident. We were all airlifted to a hospital. Everyone survived except Marcus. Except Marcus and our child." Lynn sighed heavily.

Heidi's world of stability began to collapse. What was happening? The grief, the turmoil, the heartache. She could feel her aunt's pain. Oh, why? Why did bad things happen to such good people? Tears fell freely from her eyes. She leaped up and threw her arms around Lynn.

"I'm so, so sorry." Heidi cried.

Lynn embraced Heidi and wiped her tears away. "Sweetie, I wasn't finished. I wanted to tell you that your mother helped me through the darkest time of my life. At first, it was all too much to bear, and so I moved far away to England. I couldn't stand to see your mother and father so happy in love, and then knowing that you were just adding to their happiness made me long for the life I would never have. Your father was so upset with me. He told me I was running away from my problems, and if I didn't face them, they would consume me, and I would disappear into a hollow version of myself. Of course, that upset me even more, even though he was right.

"But your mother, she never gave up on me. In fact, all those books that you read, those were from her. Every month, she would send me a book that tore at my soul. But each tear opened a spot for me to replace my heartache with hope.

"One day, I asked her to send me pictures of you. When she did, she told me she had stage four cancer and that she and your father named me as your caretaker should anything ever happen to him too. That was the second most devastating news I'd ever received. So I decided to move back to the states. I finally was settled here, and I was talking to your father about meeting you for the first time..." Lynn trailed off.

"The last thing your dad said to me was how much he missed your mother but how grateful he was that you had her strength. He said no matter what happened in your life, you would overcome it."

Heidi was overcome with emotion. Her father thought she was strong like her mother? How could she ever compare to such a wonderful being of kindness and compassion? Her mother was everything Heidi hoped to one day be.

"So, Heidi, when you tell me that a boy at school saw in you, what your father knew long ago, that makes me love you even more." Lynn kissed Heidi on the top of her head and darted off to make dinner.

Heidi sat with Toby beside her. How wonderful that the books she held so dear were bought with love and thoughtfulness from her mother. She imagined her mother picking out each one specifically geared toward what emotion Lynn was facing at the time. Her mother always believed words held power, especially the ones inspired by God.

Maybe Nick was right. Maybe Heidi could help Janice. If there is no other way but to share in her grief. That would require Heidi to step outside of her comfort zone. To breach the huge wall of anxiety that strives so desperately to keep her within its enclosure. Heidi wasn't confident of that possibility.

*****

The next day greeted Heidi with a cascade of sunshine entering her room. She could hear her mother whisper, *"Greater is He that is in you, then he who is in the world."* Heidi knew that to be true. She knew all of it to be true. However, sometimes implementing that belief into everyday life was no easy task. *"If God be for you, who could be against you?"* Heidi smiled as the memories of her mother flooded her halls of doubt.

"Heidi, sweetie. There's someone here to see you."

Heidi glanced outside her window to see a blue pickup truck. Hurriedly, she dressed and made her way downstairs. Her heart beating viciously in her chest. It couldn't be. It was.

Nick smiled at her in the doorway. "Hi. My truck is fixed, so I thought maybe I'd pick you up. If that's alright with your aunt, I mean."

Heidi stared at Lynn. "Well, I know Heidi loves to ride the bus, so—"

Heidi interrupted her. "No, it's fine. I'd rather ride with Nick." Heidi kissed her aunt as she laughed and waved them out the door. "Drive safe."

"Always do." Nick waved back as he opened the passenger door for Heidi.

Heidi reached inside her backpack and pulled out a book she grabbed from the shelf. She pulled out a pen and began to write inside:

To Janice,

    May you find peace in knowing that it does get better.

    A friend, if you need one,
    Heidi

"What's that?" Nick asked as he opened the school door for Heidi.

"Hope," Heidi said as she walked toward Janice.

CHAPTER 4

Dawson's Dilemma

Dawson grabbed Jimmy's hand as they sat on the porch. They had been best friends since kindergarten. One day, in their freshman year of high school, Dawson and Jimmy developed feelings for each other.

Dawson's parents were divorced, and his mother, Brittany, was dating a lovely lady named Lucy. Dawson never understood how his mother could go from loving his father to loving another woman in *that* way until he met Lucy. Lucy was beautiful and kind and treated his mother with adoration and respect. Two emotions his father never expressed to her.

In fact, it was his mother's relationship with Lucy that opened Dawson's eyes to love. Dawson knew he loved Jimmy. Dawson also knew it was wrong. He knew that his mother's relationship was wrong too. But hey, the world said it best, "Love is love."

Dawson also loved Jesus. Dawson came to know Jesus while attending the Summer Camp for Young Artists in his junior year. Blank canvases never stayed blank when Dawson held them in his hands. Within moments, with strokes of color whisked across the page with a flick of his wrist, a masterpiece appeared.

It was at the Summer Camp for Young Artists where Dawson met Tonya. Tonya was covered in tattoos and often allowed curse words to escape her lips. Tonya kept a mini Bible in her pocket.

That's how Dawson met Jesus—through a tall, curse word–throwing, inked brunette.

"So you in a relationship?" Tonya asked.

Dawson smiled. "Are you asking me out? If so, I'm taken."

Tonya rolled her eyes. "No, dumbass. I meant with Jesus. Do you have a relationship with him?"

Dawson hadn't known how to respond. "Um. Jesus? Like in the Bible story Jesus? Why would I have a relationship with him?"

"That's all I needed to know. Thanks." With that, she walked away.

Dawson followed her. "Hey, wait. Really? You don't even ask my name? You just ask me if I know Jesus? Who are you to ask me that, and why do you care?"

Tonya stopped and turned around to face Dawson. Her gaze traveled slowly from his feet to his face and stopped at his eyes. "I had a dream about you. That I was going to change your life."

"You had a dream about me? You don't even know me. Are you on something?"

Tonya shook her head. With two soft hands, she reached up and smacked Dawson square in the forehead. "Wake up!"

Dawson stood there, rubbing his head. "What did you do that for? Seriously, what is wrong with you?"

"I'm not the one who's wrong, Dawson." Again, she began to walk away.

"Hey!" He touched her arm. "How did you know my name? Are you psychic or something?"

"No, dumbass. You're wearing a name tag."

Dawson laughed. He looked at her shirt. "Tonya?"

Tonya smiled at him. "That's my name. Don't forget it."

Dawson would not forget her name. In fact, in the next six weeks, he learned all there was to know about Tonya Macintosh. She endured a life Dawson would not wish on his enemies. She was brought up in foster care. Two things each family had she stayed with: rapists and alcohol. Tonya had been raped six times. Once in each foster home. After the second placement and another attack, Tonya found the family liquor cabinet. She quickly learned how to drown out the pain. Until the schools noticed. Drunkenness did not sit well on a thirteen-year-old.

Finally, Child Protective Services were called one last time, and she was placed in the care of a high school science teacher. This teacher was married to a pastor. Instead of using her as a sex toy, they loved her. They enrolled her in counseling and rehab. They led Tonya to Jesus. They soon discovered Tonya had visions within her dreams. Visions that often would come to fruition. They believed this to be a gift and instructed Tonya to write them down and pray about their content.

Tonya had been sober for five years. She believed she would become a missionary until she dreamed of Dawson. Brown hair, green eyes, walking down a dead-end road. This road had mines lining the edges. With each wrong step, a mine would explode, causing Dawson to lose a piece of himself until there wasn't much left. At first, Tonya did not understand her purpose in the dream until she saw herself walking beside Dawson, picking up his pieces. She would then sprint ahead and hand them off to none other than Jesus. Jesus took Dawson's missing pieces and put him back together, just like Jesus had done with Tonya's.

"That is some deep shit," Dawson said. "So all the horror you went through, and you still chose to follow Jesus? If he truly is an all-knowing God, then where was he when you were suffering?"

"He was right there. Every second. I would dream of this white blanket that would wrap itself around me. I always felt a sense of peace amid the pain. I never realized what the dream meant until I stopped drinking. It was God. It had always been God."

During the last week of camp, the students were instructed to display their creativity in a talent show. Dawson listened as Tonya sang "Amazing Grace." Dawson's ears filled with angelic tones that caused goosebumps to travel down his spine; something stirred within his heart. A tug. A pull. A nudge. With each word that Tonya sang, Dawson felt conviction, pity, sadness, and then hope.

Dawson's creativity was displayed when he unveiled his painting. One broken soul walked a destructive path while a beautiful brunette, pieced together with love and hope, ran ahead, holding the pieces out toward Jesus.

"Tonya?" Dawson asked on the last day of camp as everyone began to load the busses to return home. "Can we keep in touch?"

"Yeah?" Tonya asked as she wrapped her arms around Dawson and grazed his lips with her own.

"You do know that I'm gay, right?" Dawson spoke those words, but at that moment, he questioned their sincerity.

"Dawson, you are who you choose to be. Here. This will help you. Don't forget me." She placed her mini Bible in his hands before disappearing onto the bus behind his. Dawson boarded his bus and sat down. His canvas beside him. He tried to give it to Tonya the night before, but she refused.

Dawson opened the tiny Bible. How had he not known this truth before? The more he read, the more he longed to know. When he came upon the scripture concerning homosexuality, Dawson paused. He closed the book. He did not want to continue. Dawson didn't like being told he was wrong. He remembered the feel of Tonya's lips. He began to read again. This time, he read the entire book. The last page held an inscription:

> Make sure the road you travel next is the Roman Road.
>
> —T'

Those six weeks changed his life and his belief system. There was no brainwashing, as some of his friends accused. There was only real, unconditional agape love. The kind of love where someone so powerful gave up everything to suffer and die a horrific death so that whoever would choose it could have a chance at eternal life. With no strings attached. There was no cost to salvation, for Jesus had already paid the price. There was only one catch: Once you accepted Jesus as your personal Savior, you would need to be willing to change.

Change. The word everyone feared. The *Oxford Dictionary* defines *change* as the act of replacing something with something else:

modifying. Making different. Dawson learned that if he truly loved Jesus, as Jesus loved him, then Dawson could not remain the same. Jesus paid the price for Dawson's sins, and if Dawson was willing, Jesus would begin to change him from the inside out. Dawson was already experiencing this. The more Dawson read the pocket Bible that was given to him, the more he began to understand that the feelings he had let consume him concerning Jimmy were not the feelings Jesus wanted him to have.

"Dawson, what's wrong?" Jimmy asked.

Dawson pulled his hand away from Jimmy's grasp. "Jimmy. I-I can't. I can't do this anymore."

"Do what?" Jimmy's eyes teared up.

"I can't be in a relationship with you. Not if I want to continue to have one with Jesus."

"Jesus! Jesus! I thought we were past this. I thought you agreed with me. Love is love. If Jesus didn't want us to be together, then why would he let us feel this way?" Jimmy touched Dawson's cheek.

Dawson stood up. "I'm so sorry, Jimmy. I'll always be your friend, but I can't keep living this way. I can't." Dawson shook his head. "I've tried. I've tried for two years, Jimmy."

Jimmy stood up and walked down the steps. "Give me a call when you figure out you want me more than your weird fetish with Jesus."

Dawson's dilemma was real. His struggle was great. The emotions that tortured him during the day invaded his dreams at night. He could still feel Jimmy's lips on his. When their relationship first turned into more than friendship, Dawson believed he had his life figured out. He and Jimmy would attend the same college, at NYU, and then they would get married. The state of New York would never judge them; it would only welcome them with open arms.

Arms. Jimmy's arms. Dawson's heart broke every time he remembered how they felt around him. Dawson grabbed the little Bible from under his bed and began to read.

> Therefore if any man be in Christ, he is a
> new creature: old things are passed away; behold,
> all things are become new. (2 Corinthians 5:17)

"I know. I know. But, God," Dawson prayed aloud, "I didn't expect this to be so hard. Why is this so hard? Jimmy has a point. If this is wrong, why do we feel this way?" Dawson's eyes skimmed through the tiny pages until his eyes landed on another scripture.

> There hath no temptation taken you, but such as is common to man: but God is faithful, who will not suffer you to be tempted above that ye are able; but will with the temptation also make a way to escape, that ye may be able to bear it. (1 Corinthians 10:13)

> Submit yourselves therefore to God. Resist the devil, and he will flee from you.
> Draw nigh to God, and he will draw nigh to you. Cleanse your hands, ye sinners; and purify your hearts, ye double minded. Be afflicted, and mourn, and weep: let your laughter be turned to mourning, and your joy to heaviness. Humble yourselves in the sight of the Lord, and he shall lift you up. (James 4:7–10)

Dawson began to sob. "This is not your way, Lord. This is my selfish act. Thank you for loving me. Please forgive me for these feelings I'm having toward Jimmy. Help me overcome them with your truth. Please. Please don't forsake me."

Dawson had remained friends with Tonya. Her email was inside the mini Bible, so he often reached out to her with questions. Tonya taught Dawson the truth about the devil.

"The truth about the devil is that there is no truth in him." Tonya had informed him. "He is a liar. The devil is the father of lies and confusion."

Even though Dawson knew that to be true, he would often forget. "Dawson, the truth is that the devil is very good at his job. His job is to steal, kill, and destroy every relationship that is rooted in Christ."

Of course, Dawson also knew that to be impossible. "If someone is truly rooted in Christ, their faith cannot be uprooted. Try as the devil might, the truth of Jesus always prevailed. Good always wins. Evil always loses, right?"

"Yes, that's correct. The problem, however, is how the world distorts the two. They call evil good and good evil."

Dawson knew his mother was lost. Trying to convince someone of their wrong living when they clung to it so tightly was almost impossible. Almost. God was an expert at making the impossible possible. God proved time and again how miracles could and would take place if one would only believe. Dawson believed in a miracle. Every day, Dawson prayed. He prayed for his mother and Lucy to find salvation. He prayed for Jimmy to forgive him and to discover the truth in Jesus. Dawson also prayed for his father wherever he was now. Dawson prayed for Tonya.

"Enough, Dawson! I don't want to hear it. I'm glad you found your peace with whatever idea you want to cling to, but that is not my peace. Got it? Your truth is not my truth. Stop shoving it down my throat!" Dawson's mother screamed.

More times than Dawson cared to admit, he sucked at telling people about Jesus.

"Dawson, I think you're going at it all wrong," Tonya emailed.

"What do you mean?"

"You have a gift. Use it. You are right. You obviously suck at talking about Jesus. So stop talking about him. Instead, paint him. Paint the truth."

"Thanks, Tonya. You're the best."

"I know. Hey, I'll be offline for a while. I'm going to do some traveling."

"Will you be getting a phone then? You're seriously the only person I know who doesn't own one."

"Why do I need a phone? Everyone who's important emails me. I cherish my peace."

"So where will you go? When can I expect you back? I need your constant guidance."

"No, you don't. You're a grown-up now in all aspects of your life. I'm proud of you, Dawson. I'll be in touch."

Months turned into years, and Dawson opened a galley in Italy. Dawson's mother divorced Lucy. Irreconcilable differences, they wrote on the papers, but Dawson knew it was because Lucy had come to know Jesus. Dawson was patiently waiting for his mother to do the same.

"Dawson," Lucy called him one night. "It's your mother. I'm sorry. She's had a heart attack."

Dawson's plane landed in Maine, and Lucy was waiting at the baggage claim. Dawson hugged her tightly. "Oh, Dawson, I'm so sorry."

"Thanks, Lucy. How are you doing?" Dawson couldn't help but feel the bump between them.

"I'm doing well. Michael is too." Lucy rubbed her protruding stomach. "This is Deanna."

"Congratulations. I'm so happy for you."

"Thank you. That means a lot."

The two of them retrieved his luggage and walked the route to Lucy's car.

"What happened?" Dawson asked.

"I'm not sure. What I do know is that the neighbor did a wellness check because he couldn't get in touch with her. The police found her on her couch, unresponsive. They tried to resuscitate her, but she was already gone."

"I wasn't aware she had heart trouble."

"When she and I were together, she began having issues. She didn't want you to worry, so we never talked about it around you. She reached out to me two weeks ago, but I wasn't available to take her call. Now I wish I had."

"Does my father know?"

Lucy shook her heard. "No one knows how to locate him. The hospital still had me listed as the person to call for an emergency." Lucy touched Dawson's shoulder. "When was the last time you spoke to your mom?"

Dawson sighed. It had been six months since their last conversation. He told her he loved her and was praying for her.

*****

"Don't pray for me, Dawson. Don't waste your breath. Your God is not my god."

"I know, Mom. But your god can't save you."

"Neither can yours." She had hung up the phone. Dawson wished he had called her right back.

*****

"There was nothing you could say or do to change her mind, Dawson. She was a very stubborn woman."

"Yes, she was." Dawson hung his head low. He knew in his heart he'd never see her again.

"Dawson, don't lose hope. You don't know what she did those last few moments. Maybe she opened her heart to him," Lucy encouraged.

"I hope so."

Brittany's memorial was well visited by family and friends. Lucy helped Dawson with all the arrangements. His mother had been a planner, so nothing was left to chance. At least nothing regarding her physical death. Dawson was grateful for the help. It was wonderful to see how many people loved his mother. He had no idea she had so many friends. She was an accountant, and Dawson learned her clients had become her friends. Everyone from Dawson's old neighborhood attended, including Samuel.

"Dawson?" a tall white-haired man stood behind him.

"Samuel. It's good to see you." Samuel lived at the end of the street. He was always kind to Dawson. Dawson would mow his lawn from time to time.

"I'm so sorry about your mother. I'm sorry I waited two days to check in on her." Tears welled up in the man's eyes. "I loved her."

"You what?" Dawson remembered how devastated his mother had been when she and Lucy divorced. Had that hurt been enough to cause her to fall for a man again?

"I loved your mother. She was my best friend. I wished we had been more, but she was very clear she did not want a relationship with me. She still loved, well, her." Samuel pointed in the direction of Lucy and her husband.

Dawson understood the pain. Part of Dawson still loved Jimmy. Jimmy had not spoken to Dawson in years. But it was a dull ache. The more Dawson grew in his relationship with Christ, the less those feelings overtook him. They were there, in the distance of his heart, but when he redirected his gaze toward Christ, they were no longer in view.

"I'm sorry for your loss as well." Dawson hugged Samuel.

Samuel nodded and walked away.

Dawson spent the next month getting the house ready to sell. After two days on the market, the house was sold. Dawson's childhood was converted into a truckload of boxes that he planned to donate. He had chosen to remain in Italy. His gallery was a success. He loved the atmosphere. He had a few friends, but mostly, he spent his time reading and painting. For a moment, he contemplated becoming a monk, but Dawson was not Catholic. He simply followed the scripture in his beloved book.

For Dawson's college graduation, Tonya had sent him an upgrade. A full-size Bible and a concordance.

"You're a big boy now," she had written. "Time to ride the bike without training wheels."

She always made him laugh. He wished he had a picture of her. Something other than his memories.

Dawson returned to Italy. He tried endlessly to contact Tonya, but the email always returned undeliverable. For months, he tried to find her on social media platforms. But Tonya Macintosh seemed not to exist. Perhaps she was a figment of his imagination? An angel sent by God to lead him in the direction of salvation?

Dawson brought in his newest painting to display for his series, titled *The Roman Road*. This series was his biggest accomplishment.

This piece showcased a young girl, pieces of her life, labeled *hurt, violation, agony*, strewn along the path she was walking. In the distance before her was a light so bright she had to drop the pieces she was clinging to and use both hands to shelter her eyes. The last broken piece she dropped was labeled *victim*.

"Impressive. Very powerful. What was your inspiration?" A soft voice caused Dawson to smile.

His finger was tapping his lips in thought. "A girl I knew once."

"A girl?" The soft voice moved next to Dawson.

"She wasn't just any girl. She was a girl who used to dream about me."

"Dream about you, huh?"

"Yes, she dreamed she would change my life." Dawson's hand dropped to his side.

"And did she?" The soft voice lowered her hand as well.

Dawson's fingers interlocked with hers. "She did." Dawson's face lit up as he turned toward her. "Hello, Tonya."

"Hello, Dawson."

The two embraced for what seemed like hours.

"What are you doing here? I tried finding you. You were nowhere."

"I was everywhere from Montreal to Mexico. Then I had to find you. I had another dream."

"Really? About me?" The joy Dawson felt from seeing Tonya spread across his chest. Happiness filled his being.

"About us." Tonya smiled.

"Tell me all about it," Dawson said as they walked arm and arm to the coffee shop around the corner.

CHAPTER 5

Remi's Rosebush

Remi Montgomery came into this world in a hospital basement during a stint of tornadoes. The wind howled. The lights flickered, and the devil lurked closely at her mother's feet, waiting to pounce. He believed this one to be his.

Remi's mother was divorced and had one son named Mason. When Remi was just shy of six years old, her mother moved them from Oklahoma to Texas. Remi once heard the lyrics to the song "God Blessed Texas" and thought God must have forgotten she had moved there, for Remi's childhood was not filled with blessings but a constant unawakenable nightmare.

One night, the devil whispered his horrific commands into Mason's ears. Mason arose from his bed and crept silently into Remi's bedroom. Remi opened her eyes wide. What was happening? Mason placed his hands around her throat, applying just enough pressure to prevent her from screaming. She tried to move beneath his weight, but the impossibility of that motion set in, and Remi's eyes released a stream of tears down her cheeks.

Her blurry gaze fixed on the blood-colored roses etched across her wall. She once picked a rose from a neighbor's rosebush, and it pierced her tender flesh. Roses appeared beautiful and dainty, but one wrong move, and they would slice into your skin as if warning you not to go any farther. Oh, how Remi wished God had created her to be a rosebush. When Mason finished, he left her room and closed the door.

Remi's grandmother, Lilian, would often pray for the little girl who came into the world during catastrophic tornados. The night Remi was born, four tornados ripped through their town and the next two over, leaving behind rubble and despair. Twelve people were killed during their rampage. Lilian knew Remi would one day be a tornado herself.

Remi would rip through the devil's schemes and stand strong and tall on a solid rock of faith. At least, that's the story Remi heard over and over again when she would visit her grandmother. Oh, if her grandmother only knew the devastation, Remi faced each night in her room. The catastrophic tornados were just the appetizer for the devil's plan for her life.

Remi would watch television shows of kidnapped children held against their will. During their time in captivity, they would always have opportunities to escape. Yet they never would. They would remain with their captor and sometimes even grow to love them.

"Remi, why must you watch that garbage?" her mother asked. "It's so sad. Those poor parents. Losing their children like that. How could they go on?"

"They eventually get rescued, Mamma. Eventually, someone comes to save them."

"Oh, honey. I am so glad that's never happened to you, my sweet girl." She cupped Remi's face in her hand and planted a kiss on her nose. "I'm off to work."

Remi shook her head. Her mother's name was Olivia. Remi had often referred to her as Oblivia when she would host pretend screaming matches inside her head. Her mother was oblivious to what was taking place right beneath her nose. Remi often wondered how her mother would react if she was told the truth. Would she hate Remi for not stopping the abuse? *Abuse*—such a cruel word for something that took place so often. Mason and his friends were never cruel to her. In fact, aside from the first year when Remi's life turned to hell, Mason remained gentle when he would come to visit her.

The years passed, and Remi became nothing more than a sex toy for her brother and his friends. She had grown accustomed to the *sleepovers* he would host. Remi was the new fad all the boys wanted to try. One day, Remi made the decision she would no longer be a pawn in their game of ecstasy. She was now the dealer. Remi would only sleep with the boys she chose and no one else.

Remi, however, was not Mason's only conquest. Oh no, Mason had many intimate encounters with women. Unfortunately for him, he was not always careful. Fate, God, or whoever did possess a sense of humor. Mason met Elaine, and into this world came Jeremiah.

Mason was forced to marry Elaine, and the three of them lived with Remi and Olivia. Remi did not mind at all. For once, sunshine scattered its rays across her heart. Jeremiah was always so excited to see Remi. His little arms would wrap around her neck. His tiny hands would squeeze her cheeks until she laughed. Finally, she had peace. Remi had a purpose.

Alas, Remi knew the sun would not shine forever. Remi was familiar with darkness. With every smile she gave away, she anticipated its arrival. There were, however, rare stints of time, like this one instance, where she was ill prepared for the earth-shattering heartbreak that was coming.

Mason and Elaine divorced. Just like that, Jeremiah was gone. Depression sprung its cold, dark hands upon Remi's brow and etched a veil of sadness over her eyes. The veil quickly turned into a heavy blanket that swallowed her up until there was nothing left but ache.

"Remi, honey, enough is enough. It is not the end of the world. You are fourteen years old. You should be happy. I don't understand this phase you are going through." Olivia grabbed Remi's ankles and pulled her out from the heap of covers she tightly clung to. A bottle of sleeping pills rolled onto the floor.

"Remi? What are these? Are these my sleeping pills? Remi?" Olivia shook Remi over and over. "Remi!"

Remi was transported to a nearby hospital. The stench of vomit and charcoal smacked her back into reality. So much pain. So many tears. Remi just wanted it all to go away. She just wanted to close her eyes and sleep. Of course, doctors don't take suicide attempts lightly, and Remi would be held for three days in the hospital's psychiatric unit.

"It's just for evaluation, Remi, honey. To make sure you are alright." Olivia kissed the top of Remi's head.

"I'm fine, Mamma. I'm fine." Remi stood up. "Let's just go home. Please, Mamma. I just want to go home."

"You will, honey. Soon. I promise." Olivia said goodbye, and Remi was left to stare at the gray walls that began to close in on her.

> The devil bounced from gray wall to gray wall. Over Remi's head. Under Remi's feet. Beside her. Whispering his lies. He was so close! So close to having her! He was very disappointed when her mother tried to wake Remi. He knew that observational skills were not Olivia's strong suit, especially regarding her daughter. He was counting on that! Ugh! That grandmother of Remi's! What nerve she had praying for such a lost cause such as Remi. He saw the angel pushing Olivia to check on her daughter, and he knew the grandmother's prayers were the culprit. But now, he had Remi alone.

Lilian cried out to the Lord, pleading, "Please, Lord. Don't let her give up. Keep her safe. Help her. She doesn't know she needs your help, but I do."

Three days later, Remi put on the fakest smile she could muster and thanked the nurses when they wheeled her to the car. Olivia smiled too.

"See, Mamma. I'm fine. I promise." Remi squeezed her mother's hand as they drove home.

While Remi was inside the gray box, she clung to the happiness she felt when she took care of Jeremiah. It took her three days to realize just how to obtain that happiness again. His name was Max. Max was twenty-one and gorgeous. He was a friend of a friend. It didn't take much coercing to convince Max to fall in love with Remi. At least, Remi's version of love. Max liked cocaine. Remi liked it too. It was a high that no amount of sex would give her. Max also liked to hit things. Remi was one of those things.

Remi could have told someone about Mason. She could have told someone about Max. But Remi did not. Instead, Remi found a bottle of sleeping pills, and this time, she was determined to use them correctly. For killing oneself, that is. What better way to accomplish this than to mix them with cocaine?

Remi fell into a coma of nothingness. Was she dead? There was nothing. No pain. No heartache. No remorse. Just nothing. Wait. What was that? Remi heard a voice calling to her. Remi's eyes opened slowly. She tried to understand what she was seeing. There were red and green flashes. No, not flashes. Round red pieces of something attached to green sticks. Remi's gaze focused. A pot of red roses sat on a table in the room she was in. It was a rosebush.

"Remi. Honey. Why are you doing this to me?" Olivia took her hand and brushed the hair from her head.

Unfortunately, Remi was not dead. "Hi, Mamma." Remi squeezed Olivia's hand.

"Remi, how could you do this to me again? And the baby…" Olivia's voice cracked.

Wait. What? Remi blinked. "Baby? What baby, Mamma?"

"Remi, you're three months pregnant. You mean, you didn't know? I thought that's why you wanted to kill yourself. Oh, Remi!"

Remi was unaware she was pregnant. She had not kept track of her monthly flow. Had she had one? She couldn't remember. Perhaps it *had* been three months since her last period.

Baby? Oh no! "Mamma. What about the baby? Is the baby okay? I didn't know. I didn't know. I would never have—if I knew—" Remi grabbed her stomach.

"The baby is fine. Thank the Lord. The baby is fine. But you obviously need help, Remi."

"Mamma, I promise. I swear. This will not happen again. I'm going to be a mother." Remi closed her eyes and drifted back to sleep.

Days turned into weeks, and weeks turned into months. Remi completed her rehabilitation and found a job cleaning houses at night. During the day, she put herself through beauty school. Remi had a way of making the homeliest person look stunning. *"You have a gift,"* Remi's grandmother would tell her. *"You can take something unappealing and turn it into something beautiful."*

Lilian went to be with the Lord two weeks before Israel was born. At least, that's what the obituary read. Remi was still uncertain if there was an afterlife. This life was hell enough. Why would anyone want to keep going when their body finally quit? Remi missed her grandmother so much. Remi wished Lilian could be there to hold Israel. He was perfect. Ten fingers. Ten toes. Dark eyes. He was breathtaking.

Remi planted the rosebush she received in the hospital. It had been from Max. She had told him about the baby. Unfortunately, a child did not fit into his five-year plan. Nor his ten-year one. Of both, Remi was ever so grateful.

Through the years, the rosebush blossomed, grew, and spread into a wall of exquisiteness. Admire from a distance. Look, but don't touch. That also became Remi's motto, and it worked. Mason never touched her sexually again. His friends stayed away unless Remi called them, which she was known to do from time to time.

Remi had given up the life of addiction where the drugs were concerned, but her hunger for love remained. She continued her voyage through the vast ocean of boys who were available to her. One steamy night in May, Mason hosted a party, and Remi decided to attend. Remi scanned the room, and her eyes locked with a dark stranger across the room. The stranger sauntered in her direction.

"Hello," said the sweetest, roughest voice Remi had ever heard.

"Hi," Remi said, staring into his dark eyes.

He held out his hand. "I'm Bruce. I work with your brother."

Remi and Bruce talked for hours. Remi laughed. Remi flirted. Remi did all she could, but Bruce never made any advances toward her. In fact, for a moment, Remi thought he may not like women at all. Not in that way. For a moment, Remi felt safe and at ease. Could this person enjoy her companionship without any physical contact? Soon, the sunrise began peaking its head over the horizon, and Remi's eyes grew heavy. She would just close them for a moment.

Remi was lying there, frozen. She wanted to scream. She wanted to run. But all she could do was stare at the roses on the wall. Remi woke with a start. She was on the couch, alone. A blanket covered her fully clothed body. Bruce had draped the blanket over her before he left. She squeezed the blanket to her chest. Was this how relationships were supposed to be? Did the man care more about the well-being of the woman than his own needs? Remi wanted to find out.

Months passed, and Remi and Bruce spent every day together. Bruce did, in fact, like women—her especially. And Remi liked Bruce. Bruce was opening the door to a world that Remi had never seen before. He had a peace within him that Remi longed to possess. She soon discovered he was a pastor's son. His peace, he claimed, came from Jesus.

Jesus. Oh, Jesus. God's only Son. Sent to die so we could live. Remi had heard the story numerous times before. She knew of God. He just chose not to know of her. If he truly cared, as her grandmother used to say, then why had he allowed all those terrible things to happen to her? Why did he not just let her die when she begged him to do so each time she had taken the pills? What reason did he have to keep her alive unless he delighted in her suffering?

"Mamma! Mamma!" Israel came running into the living room.

Remi shook her head and bent down to pick up the little boy she held so dear. Something within her stirred. "Bruce is here. Bruce is here!"

Bruce walked in behind Israel and smiled. He withdrew a small blue box from his pocket. Israel wriggled out of Remi's arms and stood beside him. "I have something I'd like to ask you."

Six months after their wedding, Bruce accepted a job out of state. Remi stood admiring her striking rosebush. Each crimson petal was slightly different from the other. Dark green stems held the delicate pieces together. Tiny thorns were placed perfectly on the stems to defend their innocence.

"Do you want to take it with us?" Bruce came behind Remi and placed his arms around her protruding stomach.

"When I was younger, I wished I was a rosebush. I wished I had thorns to ward off the animals."

Bruce turned Remi toward him and cupped her face in his hands. "Remi, my love. Have you not realized that you are like that rosebush? You are strong and beautiful, and you have overcome devastation in harsh climates, only to grow and flourish so that you can be truly cherished by those who choose to love you."

Bruce's words brought tears to Remi's eyes. There was so much depth to what he said. He didn't mention God at all, yet Remi felt God's love seeping into her soul when he spoke. She lay her head on Bruce's shoulder. Could there be such a thing as God's love? Could God love her? She had partaken in so many sinful acts of pleasure and turmoil. How could he not look at her with disgust?

Years passed, and Remi spent her time taking care of her children. Indiana finally felt like home. Remi watched through the kitchen window as Israel played with his little sister, Marigold. Though Remi's life was filled with peace and contentment, a longing began to tug inside her heart. Bruce was such a wonderful husband, father, and friend. Remi was ever grateful for his love for her. She adored the way he loved Israel as his own and the protective way he taught Marigold how to ride a bike.

Remi was aware of Bruce's love for Jesus. If Remi was honest with herself, she was slightly jealous of their relationship. It seemed almost unattainable for her. She knew the Bible was the Word of God. Bruce read from it every day. She even knew some scriptures because Bruce would post a new one every day on the bathroom mirror so he could memorize it. But he never once demanded she do the same.

Remi's thoughts were interrupted by a knock on the door.

"Hello. Mrs. Lopez?" a kind-looking man stood at her door.

"Yes?"

"I'm Pastor Ron. I saw you and your family in the church on Sunday, but you scurried away before I had the chance to say hello. I wondered if I might come in and talk to you about your relationship with Christ?"

"Relationship?" Remi asked.

"Yes, Ma'am. Relationship. That's what it's all about. Our relationship with God through Jesus Christ. Do you know him as your Lord and Savior?"

Remi thought about this for a moment. Her Lord and Savior? No. She did not. Remi invited the pastor inside and threw question after question at him. He carefully caught them and tossed back answers that began to form a picture in Remi's mind. Perhaps her salvation wasn't an illusion after all.

"Would you like to say the sinner's prayer with me? To ensure your salvation?" Pastor Ron asked.

"I think I'll pass for now. I thank you for your time, Pastor." She ushered him out the door.

> The devil danced around outside the door. He was not allowed inside Remi's home, thanks to her ever-praying husband. But he was always patiently waiting outside their door. Every time Remi ventured outside, he whispered doubts and planted discouragements inside her mind. He was slightly frustrated when she redirected her hatred for God to herself, but he had worked with that attitude before. In fact, self-loathing was his specialty. Now Remi had basically kicked the pastor out of her home! What a wonderful day! He would soon make his move one more time, and she would finally belong to him.

Remi closed the door and fell to her knees, sobbing. The image of Bruce's morning scripture kept running through her mind. *That if thou shalt confess with thy mouth the Lord Jesus, and shalt believe in thine heart that God hath raised him from the dead, thou shalt be saved (Romans 10:9).*

"God, are you listening? Do you see me? Do you love me? Could you ever forgive me?" Remi cried out in agony. "Because I've been listening. I've been seeing. I choose you. I believe, God. I believe in you. I believe in your Son. Please. Please save me."

Rays of sunshine began to spill into the room. Remi heard Israel and Marigold entering the kitchen. Remi stood up and wiped her tears away. She could not explain the overwhelming feeling of relief that washed over her. She didn't know what the future would hold, but she knew that it would not include her. At least not the person she had been. She was a different Remi. She now had hope. Remi began to read the Bible daily and placed her own post-it notes along the kitchen window. She now gazed upon the rosebush with admiration for its beauty and steadfastness. Remi was no longer a lost sheep. She was now, and forever would be, saved by the grace of Almighty God.

"Nooooooo!" The devil cried out in anger.
For he had lost, yet again.

The stories within these pages are based on life experiences defined as treacherous debacles overflowing with bad decisions and catastrophic outcomes. Yet God, in his mercy, calls out to the broken and offers a solution—Jesus Christ. Believing in him and calling upon his name to be saved causes an avalanche of ripples across the timeline the devil thought belonged to him.

ABOUT THE AUTHOR

Angela's dream was to become a ballerina, until she picked up a pen and began to write. The power of the written word transformed her world into a ballet of verse and prose. Angela's early works were published in high school literary magazines. In the late nineties, she was awarded first place in a national writing competition for MADD for her essay, "Dear Mom." She is the author of *Shades of Life*, a collection of Christian poetry. She is currently working on multiple books.

She is married to her high school sweetheart, and together they have three grown children and one grandchild.

Printed in the USA
CPSIA information can be obtained
at www.ICGtesting.com
LVHW091503081124
796065LV00003B/419